THE ROANOKE MISSING PERSONS CASE

by
Anita Larsen

Illustrated by
James Watling

CRESTWOOD HOUSE
NEW YORK

Maxwell Macmillan Canada
Toronto

Maxwell Macmillan International
New York   Oxford   Singapore   Sydney

Library of Congress Cataloging-in-Publication Data
Larsen, Anita.

The Roanoke missing persons case / by Anita Larsen. — 1st ed.
    p.   cm. — (History's mysteries)
Includes bibliographical references and index.
Summary: Discusses the mysterious disappearance of the English colony on Roanoke Island and presents three possible solutions.
    ISBN 0-89686-619-X
    1.Roanoke Colony (N.C.)—Juvenile literature. [1. Roanoke
Colony (N.C.)] I. Title. II. Series.
    F229.L37 1992
    975.6'17501—dc20   91-19524
                                                                        CIP
                                                                        AC

Crestwood House
Macmillan Publishing Company
866 Third Avenue
New York, NY 10022

Maxwell Macmillan Canada, Inc.
1200 Eglinton Avenue East
Suite 200
Don Mills, Ontario M3C 3N1

Macmillan Publishing Company is part of the Maxwell Communication Group of Companies.

First Edition

Printed in the United States of America

10   9   8   7   6   5   4   3   2   1

CONTENTS

▲▲▲▲▲▲▲▲▲▲▲▲▲▲▲▲▲▲▲▲▲▲▲▲▲▲▲▲▲▲▲▲▲▲▲

THE CASE OPENS

▲▲▲▲▲▲▲▲▲▲▲▲▲▲▲▲▲▲▲▲▲▲▲▲▲▲▲▲▲▲▲▲

In August 1590, English ships anchored off the outer banks of what is today North Carolina, in the southeastern United States. Two small boats were lowered to the water. As the men rowed the boats toward Roanoke Island, a storm struck. One boat capsized. The men in the other boat tried to help, but eight sailors were lost in the rough seas of what has been called the "Graveyard of the Atlantic."

All but John White wanted to return to the big ships where they would be safe from the storm. White wanted to go on. Three years ago, he'd left nearly 100 English colonists behind on Roanoke Island. Twice he'd fought to get back to Roanoke Island and failed. Now White had returned and desperately wanted to see the colonists again. He urged the men to row on in the gathering night.

They saw a fire blazing deep in the woods on the

island's northern end. White convinced the men that it was a signal left by the colonists of 1587. The boat was anchored opposite the fire. All night the men called and sang English hymns. One blew a trumpet. No one answered.

The next morning, the men landed on the island. Tall grass, called sea oats, grew on its sandy beach and seagulls screamed overhead. But the signal fire was only a brush fire sparked by the lightning. No one came to greet him. In single file, the men headed to the opposite shore with their muskets ready.

At the top of the bank someone had carved the letters C-R-O into a tree. Farther on, the village stood deserted and silent. They saw a new palisade fence. Carved deeply on one of its entrance posts was the word CROATOAN.

White went on alone to a cove on the island's northeastern shore. The small boats the colonists had left there three years before were gone. When White returned to the village he learned that the men had found five chests buried in a trench.

Three of the chests were White's. He'd left them there three years earlier. His books had been torn. Many of their pages had been left to rot in the weeds. He found his armor covered with rust. Everything he'd left, he found ruined.

N

ATLANTIC
OCEAN

FORTE
RALEIGH

ROANOKE
ISLAND

PAMLICO
SOUND

Three years ago, in 1587, he and nearly 100 colonists had landed on Roanoke Island. They had landed in the wrong place at the wrong time. They didn't have enough supplies to last the winter, and it was too late to plant crops. One colonist had already been killed in an Indian ambush.

The colonists asked White to return to England for supplies. White refused. He was governor of the new colony. He'd convinced most of the colonists to come. How would it look if he left them? Finally he decided to leave. In his journal he explained why.

The colonists had talked about leaving the island. In White's language of 400 years ago, they said they would "remove 50. miles further vp into the maine presently." They had the idea to move inland. But who would care for White's papers and his armor?

A small group of colonists came to White. They promised to take care of his treasures. They said they would put it in writing that they had asked him to return to England for supplies.

After White agreed, the group promised to leave signs to let him know if they moved while he was gone. They said they would carve their destination into trees and on door posts. If they left to escape danger, they would carve Maltese Crosses.

Three years later, White found no Maltese

Crosses. The colonists' boats were missing from the cove. Their only messages said they had gone to nearby Croatoan Island where the Indians were friendly. When he realized that, White decided to join them the next day.

But it was August—hurricane season. The weather forced White back to England. He tried again to return, but was unable to. In 1593, he wrote: "I leaue off from prosecuting that whereunto I would to God my wealth were answerable to my will." White had the will to return, but he had run out of money for the journey. Neither he nor anyone else would ever find the Lost Colonists of Roanoke Island.

What happened to them?

CASE FILE

▲▲▲▲▲▲▲▲▲▲▲▲▲▲▲▲▲▲▲▲▲▲▲▲▲▲▲▲▲▲▲▲

THE MISSING PERSONS

Detectives working on a missing persons case ask, Who is missing? What are they missing from? What were the patterns of their day-to-day lives? The answers to such questions usually help solve the case.

But asking these questions about the Lost Colonists has only led to more questions.

Who was actually missing? In 1593 John White compiled a list of 82 men, 17 women, 11 children and 2 infants. There were errors in his list. For example, neither the ship's Portuguese pilot Simon Fernandez nor John White stayed on Roanoke Island. Yet both were listed. And three of White's assistants never left England in the first place but were also on the list.

No one is sure where the colonists came from. At least two of them were Irish. It is thought that most of the colonists were from Devon, a county in southern England. Devon farmland was poor. Many of the men of Devon had turned to the sea for their income. Some had attacked Spanish ships full of South American gold as they returned to Europe with their plunder. These sailors were called privateers.

Devon was the home of famous *sea dogs* like Sir Francis Drake, who was part pirate and part hero. Sir Walter Raleigh, the adventurer who chartered the Roanoke colonists, was also from Devon.

Raleigh was tall, charming, and handsome enough to turn even a queen's head. Almost as soon as his half-brother Sir Humphrey Gilbert, also an explorer, introduced him to the royal court, Raleigh became the queen's favorite.

The queen wouldn't let Raleigh go on voyages. But she was happy to support the voyages he arranged for others. She was especially happy to support a voyage that might prevent Spain from controlling all of the New World.

One certainty about the Roanoke colonists was that they were Elizabethans—they represented

Elizabeth's world. Elizabethans were generally hard workers. That meant the colonists were also used to working hard. Even rich Elizabethans commonly worked from dawn until nine or ten at night. The rich did the same work that they ordered their servants to do. Servants dutifully followed orders—even when told to change their clothes!

During their free time, adults and children bowled on the grass or played leapfrog. Some played rough games using cudgels, or long, thick sticks. The rules of cudgel playing were simple: Whack your opponent; the winner is the one who draws first blood. They also played new games like tennis or they danced. Queen Elizabeth's favorite dance was the Spanish Panic. It was an active dance, and she danced it actively.

Spectator sports included bear baiting, in which fierce, trained dogs attacked a chained bear. When the bear fought back, the dogs bit and held on. The crowd came to see the gore and violence. "A goodly sight," one happy spectator went home and wrote in his journal. Other Elizabethans went to see plays by such playwrights as William Shakespeare. Many plays were violent. Often stages were littered with "dead" actors by a play's end.

The Roanoke colonists would have participated

in these entertainments in England. They would also have shared the Elizabethan way of looking at the world. Elizabethans believed that all earthly life was organized by God in a great *chain of being*. Each link in the chain fit into a hierarchy with God at the top, man in the middle, and the animals below. Queens and kings ruled by a *divine right* that came from God, not the people. That made Queen Elizabeth the top link on earth, connecting her to Heaven.

Being the top link also made her the "best" person. Nobles were the next best, then land-owners, and so on.

One sure way to be "better" was to be born into a noble family. But a person could also become better by doing something important for the nation such as starting a colony in the New World. That's why many Elizabethans took risks.

People of privilege had greater power than people below them. Once you rose up the social ladder, it was wise to let other people know it. The best way to do that was to possess an emblem of rank—a coat of arms or a suit of ceremonial armor like John White's, which he found rusted on Roanoke Island.

THE "CITIE OF RALEIGH"

The Roanoke Colony grew out of the ideas of social betterment. It was a business deal. These colonists weren't like the later Pilgrims who left England to escape religious persecution. Instead, they were crossing the ocean and starting colonies in order to rise socially. John White had a contract with Queen Elizabeth and Sir Walter Raleigh to govern the "Citie of Raleigh" in the New World. Once they'd founded a colony, White and his twelve assistants would be given coats of arms. Almost overnight, they would become socially "better."

The other colonists would gain too. A charter ensured that each man would get 500 acres of land simply "for the adventure of his person." That was more land than they could dream of owning in England.

Before they left England, the colonists felt sure their venture would succeed. But they were not convinced once they arrived. When they landed on Roanoke Island at sunset on July 22, 1587, they saw the first sign of trouble. An Englishman's skeleton lay on the shore. There was also the threat of a Spanish or Indian attack, and the dangers of the wilderness itself.

THE EARLY VOYAGES

The Roanoke Voyages had started happily three years earlier. In 1584 Queen Elizabeth gave Raleigh permission to look for and take faraway "heathen and barbarous" lands. Raleigh asked Portuguese pilot Simon Fernandez for information. Then he sent a single ship to the New World, piloted by Fernandez.

The report from this voyage was promising, so Raleigh arranged for a second voyage. Philip Amadas and Arthur Barlowe would each command a ship on this voyage, and Fernandez would be the pilot of both ships.

The Amadas-Barlowe Voyage landed close to Roanoke Island in July 1584. The place was a paradise. The voyage returned to England in September with glowing reports. Two natives, Manteo and Wanchese, sailed with them.

In October, Raleigh introduced the Indians to Queen Elizabeth. Raleigh showed the queen tobacco and potatoes, marvelous new plants from the New World. He also gave her a book that described the wonders found there.

Raleigh suggested the English colonize the area and call it Virginia, after the queen. She was flattered. Since she had never married, she was

called the Virgin Queen.

She gave Raleigh a title and support for another, larger voyage to the new colony of Virginia. Raleigh's officers were given the right to "take up," or demand men and ships for this voyage. Usually this forced draft, or conscription, was only done in wartime, and England wasn't at war with Spain—yet.

One of the conscripts to sail on Raleigh's ship was a Irishman named Darby Glande. Later, he would add a chilling twist to the story of the Lost Colony.

Queen Elizabeth was interested in supporting this voyage to Virginia because she thought North America might be as rich as South America. Spain had brought home fabulous wealth from South America. The Spaniards traveled in clusters of treasure ships called the *plate fleet.*

The Spanish plate fleet was a second reason why the queen was interested. The area would be a good base for privateers. Privateers were pirates who operated with state support. Queen Elizabeth thought privateering would profit England. Even if there wasn't as much gold in Virginia as Amadas and Barlowe reported, the Spanish plate fleet was packed with treasure from the New World. An English privateer could attack ships in the Spanish plate fleet from a base in Virginia and then sail safely back there.

In the spring of 1585, the queen sent seven ships to Virginia under the command of Sir Richard Grenville. Some of the men would stay to establish a colony and maintain a privateer base. This 108-man colony would be governed by Ralph Lane.

The voyage had serious aims. Scientist Thomas Hariot would study and list the plants and animals of the area. Artist John White, who later would become governor of the ill-fated Lost Colony, would make watercolors of the New World. Three foreign mining experts went to explore for gold. Amadas would also go back, as would Manteo and Wanchese.

Grenville's fleet was in no hurry. It even did some privateering along the way. Lane and Grenville often argued with each other. Their tempers continued to cause problems after the voyage landed south of Roanoke at the end of June.

At first, the natives were generous. They even helped the English search for gold. Then Grenville lost a silver cup and decided that an Indian had stolen it. He gave the thief a chance to return the cup. When it didn't turn up, Grenville ordered his men to destroy the natives' village.

Afterwards Grenville's fleet sailed up the coast. They came near where Amadas and Barlowe had landed the year before. To get there, Fernandez decided to take a shortcut. But the flagship of the fleet, *Tyger*, ran aground and its hull split. The ship was repaired, but the supplies it carried were ruined.

Had Fernandez taken this dangerous turn on purpose? Did he want to sabotage the flagship? Some of the sailors thought so. They muttered about Spanish spies.

Some of the muttering stopped when the Roanoke Indians came forward to help. They said Lane could establish his colony on the northern end of their island. The Englishmen also met Manteo's people, the Hatteras-Croatoans.

Grenville left for England, promising to send supplies to replace those lost when the *Tyger* ran aground. Lane's men began building a fort near a small creek, where they thought the Spanish could not see them. But Spanish records, found hundreds of years later, showed that the Spanish *had* seen them.

Lane's men also built two-story cottages between the fort and the Roanoke Indian village. Lane hunted for the pearls and gold mentioned in the

local tales. He found pearls, but the gold turned out to be copper. Lane was disappointed.

He also felt Roanoke Island was a privateer base that could not be defended. The natives told Lane about a bay 150 miles north, called the Chesapeake. That sounded better to him.

In the months that followed, food was scarce. The Indians fed everyone. Soon Lane decided that only gold or a passage to the South Seas would make Roanoke Island worthwhile. About the same time, Wanchese's loyalties returned to his own people, who were beginning to feel crowded.

By Christmas of 1585, the food shortage was life-threatening.

LANE'S TROUBLE

Roanoke Chief Wingina worked out a system of payment for food. The chief went to his mainland village and told his people not to trade with the English. Reacting angrily, Lane began taking Indian prisoners.

From one prisoner, Lane learned that Wingina planned an attack. Lane planned his own attack but had to call it off when the Roanoke Indians heard about it. So he called for a peace conference. Wingina agreed.

On June 1, 1586, Lane and 25 armed men went to the mainland. Wingina waited in the darkness with his men. An English voice shouted "Christ, our Victory!" Shots rang out, and men were hit.

To confuse his enemies, Wingina used a strategy of diversion. He fell on the bodies of his dead warriors. Then he sprang up and darted toward the woods. One of Lane's "Irish boys" fired and hit Wingina. He got up and ran on. The scientist Hariot and an Irish soldier chased and killed him. They returned, dangling the chief's head as a prize.

Lookouts had previously been sent to Croatoan Island to watch for the ships bringing Grenville's promised supplies. A week after Wingina was killed, the lookouts saw ships. But they weren't from Grenville. They were ships from Sir Francis Drake's fleet.

Drake had been out looking for Spanish treasure ships to attack. The Roanoke colonists climbed aboard Drake's ships and sailed for home. Manteo went; Wanchese stayed.

Two days later, Grenville's relief ships arrived. They didn't find anyone on Roanoke, so they took their supplies back to England.

A couple of weeks after that, Grenville's main fleet landed. Grenville and his men marched for

miles around Roanoke. They tried to find Indians who would give them news of Lane's colony. They learned nothing.

When Grenville departed from Roanoke in 1586, he left 15 men to guard the settlement until new colonists and privateers could be recruited. He left enough supplies to last the men two years. Soon after the 15 guards had settled in, the Indians ambushed them. Some of the guards tried to escape by boat to a nearby island. One of them made it only to the shore. It was his skeleton that White's colonists found on the shore the next year, in 1587.

THE LOST COLONISTS' VOYAGE

White was able to recruit colonists in spite of Lane's report of the trouble he had had with the Indians. The glowing promises in Thomas Hariot's book, *A Briefe and True Report of the New Found Land of Virginia*, overshadowed Lane's disturbing news.

Lane also told Raleigh what the Indians had said about the Chesapeake Bay. So Raleigh chartered White's colony to take possession of the land around the Chesapeake Bay, but *not* of Roanoke Island.

The colonizing voyage left Portsmouth, England,

in late April 1587. Families, single men and women and young boys sailed. One of the families was White's daughter Eleanor's. She had married Anias Dare, and the couple was expecting a baby. Irishman Darby Glande sailed too. Manteo was going back. Simon Fernandez was the pilot.

There was trouble on this voyage from the start. Fernandez and John White were like two dogs leashed together but chasing two different cats. White insisted on stopping along the English coast to take care of business details. He held up the crossing date until May 8. Fernandez was anxious to leave the waters around England so he could search for Spanish treasure ships. He didn't want to stop and search for the voyage's flyboat, a small and fast ship full of settlers that was lost early in the trip.

On July 1, the ships put in at St. John's Island in the Caribbean Sea to take on fresh water. While they were stopped, Darby Glande deserted. White's journal doesn't delve into Glande's desertion. White was more upset about Fernandez.

All their bickering came to an end 76 days after the start of the voyage. Fernandez was tired of the argument. He had the last word on July 22, 1587, when the ships anchored off Roanoke Island. Here White and 40 men prepared to sail to Roanoke

Island in the fleet's pinnace, a light sailing ship. White's party would deliver supplies to the 15 men Grenville had left to guard the settlement. White did not yet know that all the guards had been killed.

While White and his party were preparing to sail, Fernandez told them and all the colonists to leave. The sailors backed Fernandez. Amazingly, White didn't argue.

LIFE ON ROANOKE

When the colonists landed on Roanoke Island, they found the skeleton. They may have suspected that the trouble with the natives was still lurking in the woods. But they were unsure.

The only remaining friends the English had among the Indians were Manteo's people, the Hatteras-Croatoans, who lived on the coastline but hunted on Roanoke Island along with the Roanoke Indians. Trouble *was* lurking deep in the woods.

White and the colonists found Lane's settlement. They began repairing the buildings to use them for winter shelter. Then the flyboat they thought had been lost suddenly appeared. Things began to look up.

Then colonist George Howe went fishing. Indians shot 16 arrows into him and beat his head

"in peeces," as White wrote.

With Manteo's help, White tried to renew Indian relations. But he made a few serious mistakes.

White went to visit Manteo's people. They asked for proof that White's settlers would not steal their food as Lane's men had done the year before. They told White how the Roanokes had ambushed Grenville's settlement guards.

White invited the Croatoans to come to Roanoke in seven days for a peace meeting. They agreed. White sailed back to Roanoke and waited. The Croatoans did not come.

White decided there was only one course of action left to him. The next day, "being the ninth of August, in the morning so earely, that it was yet darke," as he described it, he and his men crossed to the mainland. They landed near the Roanokes' village and crept through the thick woods. They attacked and killed some of what White called "savages."

But he attacked friendly Croatoans, not hostile Roanokes. The Croatoans had stopped to collect food the Roanokes left behind when they fled after killing George Howe.

Manteo was upset. White quickly soothed him. Manteo told his people it was their own fault they'd been attacked. He said it was because they were late for the peace talk. Then Indians and English went to Roanoke to talk peace.

Several days later, on August 13, Manteo was christened. On August 18, White's granddaughter Virginia Dare was born. She was the first white child known to be born in what would become North America.

Soon White's campfire pact with the colonists was sworn. When White left to bring supplies from England, he carried home with him the last letters written by the colonists.

WHITE RETURNS TO ENGLAND

In England, White found the nation feverishly preparing to meet the mighty Spanish Armada. In 1588 King Philip II of Spain sent 130 ships, 2,500 guns and 30,000 men to England's southern coast. A small force of English ships met the Armada and stopped it! Only 5,000 Spaniards returned home. England lost less than 100 men and not a single ship.

But that decisive defeat did not stop England and Spain from battling at sea. The number of sea battles grew, not letting up until around 1596. In fact, all the time the Roanoke settlers were in the

New World, Spain and England were fighting.

Spanish records found centuries later report evidence of a large party of English at Port Ferdinando. They saw a slipway for loading and repairing ships, some rain barrels sunk into the sand to collect drinking water and other debris. Most experts think this was what remained from Lane's 1585 colony. But the Spanish thought there was an English settlement on Roanoke in 1588.

Some time after Darby Glande deserted in 1587, he became a soldier in the Spanish garrison at San Augustin, Florida. Glande told the Spanish officers about a large English settlement on Roanoke Island. The Spanish officers had information that confirmed the presence of English settlers. But their information placed them on Chesapeake Bay. The exact location of the English settlers was not clear. But the Spanish officers asked King Philip II for troops to destroy the English anyway. Philip refused because his attention was focused on his Armada's invasion of England.

By 1590, the colonists had vanished.

English attempts to find them went on for years. In 1602 Raleigh sent a search voyage to Virginia. It was unsuccessful. In 1607 the Jamestown settlers asked questions about the colonists. Captain John

Smith, who governed Jamestown, published a book in 1608 called *True Relations*. In it, Smith said an Indian told him that he knew where strange people lived. These people wore clothes the same as Smith's own, and not the deerskins the natives wore. Other Indians drew a map that showed that the people lived in the old territory of the Hatteras-Croatoan Indians on the mainland. Smith sent two men with the Indian to find these people. The party did not find them, but reported seeing freshly carved crosses and messages on trees. They also brought crosses and other English objects found in the area when they returned to Jamestown.

In the late 1890s, a United States census taker reported a tribe in North Carolina who called themselves the Croatans. The story of the Lost Colonists appeared in their legends and traditions. Unlike other Native Americans, many Croatans had gray eyes and many of the men had beards. The census report included colonists' names like Howe and Dare among this tribe. But not all the colonists' names appeared. Many names from White's list were missing.

In 1610 historian William Strachey stumbled upon a possible solution to the case. He wrote that he'd found two-story stone houses along Chesa-

peake Bay. Natives told him that the Roanoke settlers had taught them to build such houses. He also found out that all but seven of the settlers had been killed by a local Indian chief. The seven survivors had fled up the Chowan River to live peacefully with other natives there. This is all we know of the Lost Colony.

You have just read the known facts about one of HISTORY'S MYSTERIES. To date, there have been no more answers to the mysteries posed in the story. There are possibilities, though. Read on and see which answer seems the most believable to you. How would you solve the case?

SOLUTIONS

▲▲▲▲▲▲▲▲▲▲▲▲▲▲▲▲▲▲▲▲▲▲▲▲▲▲▲▲▲▲▲▲▲

DESTROYED BY THE SPANISH

Sea battles between the English and the Spanish went on long after the English defeat of the Spanish Armada in 1588. Spanish records show they thought there was an English settlement on Roanoke Island that same year. The officers at the Spanish garrison in San Augustin suspected there was another English settlement along Chesapeake Bay and requested troops from King Philip II to destroy the English in the New World.

The King refused to send more troops, but a small Spanish force left from Florida. They found and destroyed the "Lost Colonists" just as the settlers were sailing to Croatoan Island. This accounts for the boats that were missing from the cove in 1590. Or perhaps the colonists and their boats were lost in another sea battle with the Spanish.

DESTROYED BY INDIANS

The colonists staying on Roanoke Island soon recognized that they needed protection from the Indians. The Indians had killed George Howe even before White returned to England in 1587. After that, things went from bad to worse.

The colonists built the new palisade wall to protect themselves—the wall that White found in 1590. But since the colonists had few supplies, they had to search for food or grow it. As they did so, hostile natives ambushed them one by one. Finally, those who remained fled in their small boats to Croatoan Island for safety.

But there was little food there. And the Croatoan Indians remembered the harsh treatment given them by Lane's colony. They also recalled White's ambush while they foraged for food in the Roanokes' mainland village. Angered, the Croatoans kept their food for themselves. The remaining colonists soon starved to death or were killed.

"REMOV'D INTO THE MAINE"

The messages White found on Roanoke when he returned in 1590 didn't mean that the colonists were moving *to* Croatoan Island. They were moving inland *with* the Croatoans. Information found by the Jamestown search party in 1607 supports that theory. A comparison of John White's list of colonists' names with the U.S. government census reports in the late 1800s also proves that the Roanoke colonists had married into the Croatoan tribe.

As late as 1941, a government census report showed that 15,000 Croatans still lived in Pembroke, North Carolina. Perhaps among them were descendants of the lost colonists of Roanoke Island.

Historian William Strachey's discovery of the two-story stone houses on Chesapeake Bay doesn't disprove this solution. It would not be surprising if some Roanoke settlers had moved north to the Chesapeake Bay, while others moved inland to live with the Croatoans. They soon became known as the Croatans.

CLOSING THE CASE FILE
▲▲▲▲▲▲▲▲▲▲▲▲▲▲▲▲▲▲▲▲▲▲▲▲▲▲▲▲▲▲▲▲▲

Closing the file for this case is difficult. John White's journal is the only fairly complete account of the events, and it tells mostly about White's feelings with scant mention of fact.

Much material has been lost. What we know about the charter for the City of Raleigh, for example, comes from second-hand reports written by scientist Thomas Hariot. He mostly described the business arrangements, such as the promise of 500 acres "for the adventure of" a colonist's going.

In the last pages of his *Briefe and True Report*, Hariot said he would write about events during the time of Lane's colony. That report is missing. Did Hariot ever write it?

If so, could it have been destroyed? Elizabeth I died in 1603. The new King, James I, was interested in securing his rulership. He took a dim view of

Raleigh, a power in an earlier reign. He found Raleigh guilty of treason, threw him in prison and eventually beheaded him. King James may have destroyed a report that put Raleigh in a good light.

Also lost are the colonists' letters that White carried home when he returned to England in 1587. The letters could have revealed much about what the settlers were thinking and planning.

Reports from English privateers in the years after 1587 are also missing. In fact, English records offer little about the Virginia settlement from 1590 to 1600. The only new information in that decade was the list of colonists' names White wrote in 1593, which is faulty.

But more information could be found. Spanish records for those times still have not been completely searched. And missing objects and clues have an eerie way of unexpectedly turning up.

One surprising turn of events has already happened. White's original watercolors were lost. Copies of them were published in a book in 1590. The book was so important it was printed seventeen times and translated into four languages. But his work was lost until 1866. It had somehow been misplaced in the British Museum.

An absolute solution to this case may never be

found. But the case continues to intrigue people.

In 1653 Indians on Roanoke Island showed a group of travelers the ruins of what they called Sir Walter Raleigh's fort. Fifty years later, writer John Lawson found old coins and guns on the fort site.

Perhaps in the passing years, clues on Roanoke Island were picked up by souvenir hunters. Some clues may have vanished along with portions of the island itself. The tug and pull of the sea and storms is so strong that when the colonists arrived, Roanoke was 16 miles long. Now, worn down by time and erosion, it is only 12 miles long.

Archaeological investigation and reconstruction did not begin until the 1950s, when Lane's fort was restored. Today, the fort is a National Historic Site, run by the National Park Service.

CHRONOLOGY

▲▲▲▲▲▲▲▲▲▲▲▲▲▲▲▲▲▲▲▲▲▲▲▲▲▲▲▲▲▲▲▲▲▲▲▲▲

1584   Amadas-Barlowe Voyage lands close to
        Roanoke Island; returns to England with
        a report that intrigues Queen Elizabeth.

1585   Grenville voyages to Virginia.
        Lane's colony is established on
            Roanoke Island.

1586   Lane's colony attacks and kills Wingina.
        Roanoke Indians ambush and kill
            Grenville's settlement guards.

1587   Colonists are chartered for
            Chesapeake Bay.
        Colonists sail and land on Roanoke Island.

1588   England defeats the Spanish Armada.
        The Spanish see evidence of English
            settlement on Roanoke Island.

1590   August 17, John White returns to Virginia.
        August 18, White discovers his colonists
            are missing from Roanoke Island.

1593	John White gives up the search for the Lost Colony.
1602	Raleigh sends an unsuccessful search voyage.
1603	Queen Elizabeth I dies. James I takes the English throne.
1607	Jamestown is established.
1618	Raleigh is beheaded on a charge of treason.
1950s	Lane's fort is restored by archaeologists.

RESOURCES

▲▲▲▲▲▲▲▲▲▲▲▲▲▲▲▲▲▲▲▲▲▲▲▲▲▲▲▲▲▲▲▲▲▲

SOURCES

Byrne, M. St. Clare. *Elizabethan Life in Town and Country*. New York: Barnes and Noble, 1961.

Morison, Samuel Eliot. *The European Discovery of America: The Northern Voyages A.D. 500-1600*. Vol. 1. New York: Oxford Univ. Press, 1971.

Quinn, D. B., ed. *The Roanoke Voyages 1584-1590*. 2 vols. London: Map Library, British Library, Hakluyt Society, 1955.

Wallace, Willard M. *Sir Walter Raleigh*. Princeton, New Jersey: Princeton Univ. Press, 1959.

Weeks, Stephen B. "The Lost Colony of Roanoke: Its Fate and Survival," *Papers of the American Historical Association*, 107 (1891): pp. 441-480.

Wright, Irene A. *Further English Voyages to Spanish America 1583-1584: Documents from the Archives of the Indies*. London: Map Library, British Library, Hakluyt Society, 1951.

FURTHER READING FOR YOUNG READERS

Campbell, Elizabeth A. *The Carving on the Tree*. Boston: Little, Brown, 1968.

Stanley, Diane and Peter Vennema. *Good Queen Bess*. New York: Four Winds Press, 1990.

INDEX

▲▲▲▲▲▲▲▲▲▲▲▲▲▲▲▲▲▲▲▲▲▲▲▲▲▲▲▲▲▲▲▲▲▲▲▲▲